Grey Wolves of the

German U-BOAT Type VII

Heinz J. Nowarra

SCHIFFER MILITARY HISTORY

West Chester, PA

At left: A U-Boat VII C sets out. The U-Boat mother ship is in the background.

Bibliography:
Rössler, *Entwicklung des U-Boot-Typs VII C*
Herzog, *Die deutschen U-Boote 1906-1945*
Busch-Forstner, *Unsere Marine im Weltkrieg*
Gröner, *Die deutschen Kriegsschiffe und ihr Verbleib 1939-45*
Weyers Taschenbuch der Kriegsflotten 1941-42

Photo Credits:
Bundesarchiv, Koblenz
Nowarra Archives
Scheibert Archives

Cover Artwork by Steve Ferguson, Colorado Springs, CO

BEAR TO PORT
Cruising northeastward, only sixty miles off Cape Hatteras, North Carolina, the *Käpitanleutnant* of a lone VII-C hunter signals a shallow port turn to maintain visual contact with a merchant convoy silhouetted against the evening sky. The U-boat will stalk its prey until dark, later meeting up with other U-boats in the area. Using their infamous wolf pack tactics, they will torpedo the hapless freighters under cover of the winter night, far out in the Sargasso Sea.

The splinter camouflage patterns varied greatly and are typical of the 1941-42 winter campaign for any number of type VII-C's.

Translated from the German by Edward Force.

Printed in the United States of America.
ISBN: 0-88740-401-4

This title was originally published under the title, *Graue Wölfe auf allen Meeren - U-VII*, by Podzun-Pallas Verlag, Friedberg.

We are interested in hearing from authors with book ideas on related topics. We are also looking for good photographs in the military history area. We will copy your photos and credit you should your materials be used in a future Schiffer project.

Published by Schiffer Publishing, Ltd.
1469 Morstein Road
West Chester, Pennsylvania 19380
Please write for a free catalog.
This book may be purchased from the publisher.
Please include $2.95 postage.
Try your bookstore first.

UB-I boat of the Flanders Submarine flotilla. Its commander was Hans Valentiner, the first to have eyes painted on his boat. Other commanders soon followed his example.

The beginning of submarine construction goes back to 1848, when the Bavarian artilleryman Wilhelm Bauer first built an underwater craft. At that time, though, technology was not equal to the task; the boat sank on its first test run in Kiel Harbor in 1851. Only in 1901 was a contract given to the Krupp-Germania Shipyards for the first German submarine, U-1. It was a double-hulled boat for limited coastal defense, and was equipped with Körting oil-burning engines. On December 14, 1906 it entered the Imperial Navy, commanded by *Kapitänleutnant* von Böhm-Bezing. The picture shows U-1 off Kiel.

U-Boat Type VII

The history of this most frequently built German type of U-Boat, of which 693 were built, began —precisely speaking — on March 29, 1915, when the Flanders Submarine Flotilla was established, under the command of *Korvettenkapitän* Bartenbach.

One can still regard this man, as will be explained later, as the spiritual father of this type. At that time, small so-called coastal U-Boats were needed in Flanders. Thus the first UB-Boats came into being. As the first of its class and of the Flanders Flotilla, UB 4 sank the British steamer "Harpalyce" (5950 tons) on April 10, 1915.

The first UB I boats were so-called single-hull boats with a water displacement of 127 tons on the surface and 142 tons below. They can be regarded as forerunners of the navy's Type II, the so-called "dugout canoes."

The Type UB II originated somewhat later; these were also single-hull boats, but with 263-274/292-302-ton displacement. Finally the Type UB III was built, a double-hull type displacing some 510 to 650 tons. One of the most successful boats of this class was His Majesty's U-Boat 49, under the command of *Kapitänleutnant* von Mellenthin, who was awarded the Pour le Merite medal for his sinkings, most of which occurred in the Mediterranean. After World War I it was sent to South America. The Type UB III became the model for the new Type VII of the German Navy in World War II.

After the defeat of 1918 there were no German submarines, for according to the Treaty of Versailles Germany could not only any U-Boats. The Reichsmarine of the Weimar Republic had no intention of giving up the further development of this weapon, which even the enemy had feared and

Upper left: U-59 was one of the small Type II C coastal boats with which the German U-Boat fleet was first supplied.

Lower left: UA was a large minelaying boat that was built in 1939 and intended for Turkey. It was taken over by the German Navy and saw front service until May of 1944. It was sunk at Kiel in 1945.

Below: U-35 (Type VII A) was built by the Germania Shipyards at Kiel in 1936-37. It was lost as early as November 29, 1939, sunk by depth charges from the British destroyers "Kingston", "Kashmir" and "Icarus" northwest of Bergen.

regarded as first-class. As early as 1925, the Reichswehr Ministry set up the A-u Committee under Rear Admiral Spindler. On the basis of a study by Mellenthin, they at first took the designs of the old UB III and UC III boats as their starting point for new designs that were to be finalized in Holland. Several new projects were developed later, until the Finnish U-Boat "Vetehinen" (493-715 tons) and the Spanish E 1 (750 tons) were built and tested. The Naval Department of the Reichswehr set up a disguised U-Boat design office, "Engineering Office for Economy and Technology", or "Igewit" for short, in which the design of a 250-ton U-Boat was completed, later to be built for Finland as VC 707. This boat, which joined the Finnish Navy under the name of "Versikko", was the prototype for the new Type II. The 750-ton boat built for Spain was designated Type I.

Immediately after 1933 the construction of a German U-Boat fleet began. The "Shipbuilding Replacement Plan" of April 19, 1934 called for the building of 48 250-ton and 24 750-ton submarines by 1949. Since disguise was still necessary at that time, U-Boat production proceeded under the name of "motorized experimental boats." Four further concepts were suggested, but a design for a middle class, more or less corresponding to the UB III, was

not included. Meanwhile a new department, BU, had been established in the Reichswehr Ministry, directed by *Kapitän zur See* Bartenbach.

At a BU conference led by Bartenbach on January 10, 1935, a 550-ton U-Boat under the designation of "motorized experimental boat" (MVB) VII was advocated. Barely a week later, the Germania Shipyards in Kiel were notified that, if possible, six boats of this type were to be built. Construction was not to begin before June 1, 1935, delivery was to begin a year later and be finished by mid-1937. Naval Architect (Retired) Schürer of Igewit directed the design work and was clearly influenced by the UB III design of World War I. The boat looked much like VC 707. Otherwise, MVB VII was neither a single- nor double-hull craft, but a combination of the two. The diving cells were partly outside the ship, but the main diving cell was inside the pressure hull. This type of design was called the "saddle-tank type." Its armament consisted of four bow torpedoes and one stern tube built into the upper deck. The intended deck weapons were an 88mm rapid-fire C 35 gun and a C 30 anti-aircraft machine gun.

Type VII A

Above: The sister ship U-36 was also lost in the first year of the war. On December 4, 1939 the boat was sunk by the British submarine "Salmon" (670-970 tons). The "Salmon" was sunk by German naval forces in 1940.

After Hitler made it known on March 14, 1935 that a German air force had already existed since March 1 of that year, he announced, on March 16, 1935, the rejection of Article 173 of the Treaty of Versailles and the reestablishment of universal military duty. Just two weeks later, contracts were given to the Germania Shipyards in Kiel and the Deschimag in Bremen for a total of ten Type VII boats. The keels were laid late in 1935 and early in 1936. Without a model boat having been built, these ten boats were finished in eight months. These boats, designated Type VII A, were numbered from U-27 to 32 and U-33 to 36. They attained a surface speed of 16.5 and an underwater speed of 8 knots (1 knot or nautical mile = 1852 meters per hour). Their diving depth was 100 meters, with a maximum of 200 meters. The crew consisted of 44 men.

At the beginning of 1936, the German Navy had the small coastal U-Boats (250 tons), the large Type O A (750 tons), and the new Type VII. The Chief of the fast-growing U-Boat fleet was *Kapitän zur See Karl Dönitz*, the *Führer der U-Boote* (Leader of the U-Boats). Dönitz was an experienced submariner, who had been first watch officer and then commander of U-Boats from 1914 to 1918. On October 4, 1918 his boat, UB 68, was destroyed in the Ionian Sea, and he became a British prisoner of war. UB 68 had also been a UB III type. So it is not surprising that the new FdU declared that only Type VII would continue to be built. Types II A and II B were only suitable for coastal service, and he rejected the big Type I A because of technical difficulties.

A lucky ship was U-29, which also belonged to Type VII A. This photo was taken from U-43, commanded by *Kapitän-leutnant* Ambrosius, on July 1, 1940, and shows U-27 sinking the Greek freighter "Adamastos" in the Atlantic west of Spain. Under the command of *Kapitänleutnant* Schuhart, the boat had already sunk the British aircraft carrier "Courageous" (22,500 tons) after a two-hour pursuit in the western part of the English Channel. It was the first warship to be sunk by a submarine in World War II.

Left: Alarm! Flood the tanks! A quick dive as enemy destroyers approach.

Lower left: After sinking the "Courageous", *Kapitänleutnant* Schuhart and the LI (Chief Engineer) of U-29 relax in port.

Below: *Kapitänleutnant* Schuhart reports his success. At right are the FdU, *Kapitän zur See* Dönitz, and *Admiral* Raeder. Behind Hitler are Schuhart's flotilla chief, *Korvettenkapitän* Hartmann, and *General* Keitel. U-29 also sank eleven ships, total tonnage 62,766 tons, and was then withdrawn from front service and used only for training. She was sunk by her crew at Flensburg on May 5, 1945.

Right: A Type VII A boat being overhauled in port during the winter of 1939-40. The stern torpedo tube, mounted above the waterline, is easy to see.

The Type VII could dive in 30 seconds! In addition, tests proved it to be a reliable and safe weapon with a remarkably high fighting power in terms of its size. The only thing that bothered Dönitz was the small range of 6200 nautical miles at an average speed of 10 knots. Thus the Type VII B was developed, of which U-45, 46 and 51 were built in 1938. In this type, the range was increased to 6500 nautical miles at an average speed of 12 knots. The top speed was 17.2 knots above and 8 knots below water.

Three of the VII A boats were lost in 1939, but only one of the VII B; in 1940 three VII A and seven VII B; in 1941 no VII A but five VII B (including Prien's U-47, which was sunk on March 8, 1941 in the North Atlantic south of Iceland by the British destroyer "Wolverine." In 1942 no VII A boats were lost (all were presumably used for training), but two VII B boats were lost. In 1943 the VII A boat, U-34, was lost when it collided with a tanker near Memel, but it was salvaged and taken out of service only a year later.

The launch of one of the first Type VII B boats at the Krupp-Germania Shipyards in Kiel.

Type VII B

Of the VII B boats, U-45 to U-55 and U-99 to U-102 were built at the Germania Shipyards in Kiel, U-73 to U-76 at Bremer Vulcan in Vegesack, and U-83 to U-87 at the Flender Shipyards in Lübeck.

The VII B boats proved to be a successful design. In the first convoy battle of World War II, U-46, 47, 48, 99, 100, 101, and the Type IX boats U-38 and U-123 took part. This battle took place on October 17-20, 1940 before North Channel and was directed against the British convoys SC-7 and HX 79. In the first night, six boats sank 77,780 tons of SC-7 ships. Later 12 ships of HX-79, with 75,069 tons, were sunk. The total score was 31 ships with 152,849 tons. U-48, which took part in this battle, was the most successful U-Boat of all in the Second World War. She went into service on April 22, 1939, joined

Above: A special type of success was scored by the VII B boat U-47. Commanded by *Kapitänleutnant* Günther Prien, the boat entered the British fleet base at Scapa Flow on October 14, 1939. Only a few ships were anchored there, and the old battleship "Royal Oak" was sunk.

In the photo, U-47 is greeted by the battleship "Bismarck" after returning from Scapa Flow. The crew of the "Bismarck" came to the rail to greet her.

Right: *Kapitänleutnant* Prien (in the dark coat) with the crew of U-47; beside him is his watch officer, *Leutnant* Endrasz, later a successful U-Boat commander himself.

After several successful sorties, U-47 was sunk by the old British destroyer "Wolverine" (1120 tons, built 1919) south of Iceland on March 8, 1941. Prien and the whole crew were lost.

Left: The symbol of U-47, the "Steer of Scapa Flow", was adopted by the other boats of the 7th Submarine Flotilla. Here it can be seen on the tower of U-47.

Below: The captain of a Portuguese steamer stopped by U-47 comes on board the boat to have his ship's papers checked.

U-101 on a training cruise in the Baltic Sea. The boat was originally called U-71, was taken out of service, after several sorties, on October 21, 1943 and used only as a school ship. It was scuttled by its crew near Neustadt, Holstein on May 3, 1945.

the 7th Submarine Flotilla and, under the command of *Kapitänleutnant* Herbert Schultze, *Korvettenkapitän* Rösing and *Kapitänleutnant* Bleichrodt, all of whom were honored with the Knight's Cross, sank 51 merchant ships with 310,007 tons and one escort ship, and damaged four more ships with 29,376 tons, on 12 sorties from September 1939 to June 1941. The watch officer of all three commanders, *Oberleutnant zur See* Reinhardt Suhren, later the commander of U-564 (Type VII C), received the Knight's Cross on November 3, 1940, while still a watch officer. After August of 1941, U-48 was used only as a school and training ship, and was scuttled at Neustadt, Holstein on May 3, 1945.

The torpedo armament remained the same as the VII A boats, but the deck armament was upgraded

Part of training was going alongside a supply ship. At left, the commander carefully maneuvers U-101 into position. Two men stand at the boat's bow, ready to take the lines.

Flying boats were the U-Boats' indispensable helpers. Here a Blohm & Voss Bv 138C reconnaissance plane meets a VII C boat off the Norwegian coast.

A view of the tower of VII B boat U-86 from above. At left are the 20mm anti-aircraft gun mount and the extended antenna. At right, the sea tube is partly extended and the barrel of the anti-aircraft gun can be seen.

The most successful U-Boat of World War II, U-48, runs in to the Lorient support base on September 25, 1940, flying nine victory flags to show the number of ships she has sunk.

Above: A VII B boat in service.

Left: *Kapitänleutnant* Heinrich Bleichrodt, commander of U-48 and U-109, received the Knight's Cross October 24, 1940 and the Oak Leaves September 23, 1942.

Right: *Kapitänleutnant* Reinhardt Suhren, Watch Officer of U-48, later commander of U-564 (Type VII C), received the Knight's Cross on November 4, 1940, the Oak Leaves on January 3, 1942 and the Crossed Swords on September 2, 1942.

Left: Taking on torpedoes was one of the hardest, most dangerous jobs for the U-Boat crews in port. The precise positioning of the one-ton "eels" demanded strength and expertise of the man (U-48).

Right page: U-123, one of the two IX B boats that took part in the first convoy battle on October of 1940, with a VII B boat behind it. U-123 was taken out of service at Lorient on June 17, 1944 and scuttled there by its crew on August 18, 1944, later raised and used for several years after the war by the French Navy as the "Blaison."

Below: U-51 (Type VII B) was sunk in the Bay of Biscay, west of Nantes, by the British submarine "Cachalot" on August 20, 1940.

Lower left: A Type VII B school ship of the Danzig U-Boat School leaving Danzig Bay.

U-86 (Type VII B) on a practice run in the Baltic Sea. The boat is being taken to diving depth when not in motion as a test. The Type VII boats could disappear from the surface in thirty seconds.

several times. The 88mm gun was kept, but the machine gun was replaced by one 37mm and two 20mm anti-aircraft guns. In all, 24 Type VII B boats were built: U-45 to 55, U-73 to 76, U-83 to 87 and U-99 to 102.

Of these VII B boats, U-73, 83, 84, 86 and 87 were lost in 1943. By 1944 the U-Boats of this type were no longer in front service. Only U-28 was lost through a crew error while being used in schooling. By 1945, the VII A boats U-29 and 30 and the VII B boats U-46, 48, 52 and 78 were still afloat. They were scuttled by their own crews that year.

Typical days on Type VII B boats:

Above: the tower of U-86; behind it is a telescopic mast with a crow's nest, which was later eliminated.

Upper left: The watch officer (right) and helmsman in the tower while on the surface. Things were seldom this peaceful in the first years of the war.

U-46 was one of the VII B series (U-45 to U-55) built at the Germania Shipyards. The boat was in service during the entire war and was scuttled by her crew in Kupfermühlen Bay on May 4, 1945. The death's-head (Totenkopf) emblem was also carried by other U-Boats.

A naval war correspondent during filming on the high seas.

Type VII C

In 1938 the Type VII B was redesigned to become VII C. This was the most frequently built German U-Boat type; 659 of this type and its successor, the VII C-41, were built in all. While an extension of the range brought about the redesigning in the case of the VII B (enlargement by 120 cbm, lengthening by two meters, larger saddle cells), in the case of the Type VII C it was the planned installation of a so-called S Device, an active sonar system. For this purpose, the central part of the boat afore and abaft the tower had to be lengthened, making the whole boat 0.60 meters longer.

In addition there were various improvements, such as enlarging the tower by 60mm in width and 30 cm in length and enlarging the interior fuel tank by 5.4 cbm; there were also improvements to the lubrication and electrical systems and the diving capability. The crew and armament remained the same; only the anti-aircraft guns had to be upgraded again. The displacement was 769 tons above and 871 tons below water. The boats were 67.10 meters long and had a diameter of 6.2/4.7 meters. The engines produced 2800 HP on the surface and 750 HP underwater. The normal diving depth was 150 meters, with a maximum of 280 meters. The fuel supply was 114 tons. The top surface speed was 17 knots, underwater speed 7.6 knots. The range was 6100 to 6500 nautical miles at an average speed of 12.8 knots.

The major convoy battles on the North Atlantic were carried out through cooperation between the Luftwaffe and the Navy. The Focke-Wulf Fw 200 C's of Kampfgeschwader 40 prepared the way splendidly for the U-Boat packs. Here a squad of Fw 200 C-4 planes underway to look for enemy transport ships. Below is a Type VII B school ship at Danzig.

One of the most successful U-Boat commanders was *Kapitänleutnant* Otto Kretschmer, whose VII B boat, U-99, was torpedoed by the old British destroyer "Walker" (1100 tons, built 1917-18), in the north Atlantic southeast of Iceland. Kretschmer survived and was taken prisoner.

U-443 belonged to the first series of Type VII C, which were built by the Schichau Shipyards of Danzig. The boat saw service mainly in the Mediterranean. While attempting to disturb Allied supply lines after their landing on Algeria and Tunisia, the boat was sunk by the British warships "Bicester", "Lamerton" and "Wheatland."

After the successful conclusion of the French campaign in 1940, more and more U-Boats were transferred to the Atlantic coast. Brest, St. Nazaire and Lorient became the new homes of the submarine flotillas. Many U-Boat bunkers were built by the Todt Organization and soon became targets of British bombing attacks.

Right: VII B and C boats in the locks at Wilhelmshaven.

Lower right: Lockheed "Hudsons" of the British Coastal Command, constantly observed the movements of the German U-Boats, and caused them a great deal of trouble and destroyed many of them in bomb attacks.

Below: The emblem of the 9th U-Boat Flotilla was the red "laughing swordfish." This is the boat of Knight's Cross winner *Kapitänleutnant* Lehmann Willenbrock (left). Right

Left page, above: Three boats at the quay in Brest. The entrances to the U-Boat bunkers can be seen in the background.

Below: A VII C boat leaves the quay in Brest to advance on the enemy. As of 1943, most boats did not return.

Far left and this page: In June of 1942, U-132 (Type VII C) left the French harbor of La Pallice in ideal weather, bound for Atlantic operations.

At slow speed, the boat glides across the seldom-calm sea. The commander and watch officer observe the next boat, from which these pictures were taken. The gun crew stands ready for action at the 88mm cannon. The 20mm anti-aircraft gun is also ready, for in this area one had to be ready for attacks from the British Coastal Command at any time.

U-89 is seen here leaving the U-Boat bunker in Brest at slow speed to take part in Atlantic operations in the autumn of 1942. U-89 continued to see action in the Atlantic until it was sunk on May 14, 1943 in the central North Atlantic by the combined efforts of Catalina flying boats and the British warships "Biter", "Broadway" and "Lagan."

Two 20mm Flak 38M II in double naval mount 43 U and one 37mm Flak 42 in naval mount 43 U. Instead of the 37mm, a 20mm quadruple Flak 38/43 U or a 37mm twin Flak 42 could be installed in naval double mount 42 U. As of the end of April, the boats were no longer issued 88mm cannons, since there was no longer any possibility of using them. Only the boats stationed in the Arctic Ocean and Mediterranean Sea could keep this type of gun on request. As of July 1943, no boat could put out to sea without double Flak 28 guns. In addition, shields were mounted to protect the gun crews. Like U-441, U-256, 621, 211, 953, 271 and 263 were rebuilt as anti-aircraft submarines, which in

U-132 off La Pallice. This boat still has the simple anti-aircraft guns of 1942: a 20mm Flak 38 in a naval mount. These boats could also be loaded with fourteen mines instead of torpedoes.

practice had only defensive assignments (convoy duty).

The normal anti-aircraft equipment of the VII C boats consisted of a 20mm C/30. As of mid-1942 a quadruple MG 34 unit (7,9 mm caliber) was added. U-84 (VII B) had, besides the standard 20mm Fla C/38, an additional 20mm position behind the bridge, U-81 (VII C) had an enlarged bridge and an Italian 13 mm anti-aircraft twin machine-gun unit.

In 1943 the VII C boats were equipped with the so-called "winter garden", a second 20mm position more or less under the usual 20mm anti-aircraft gun position.

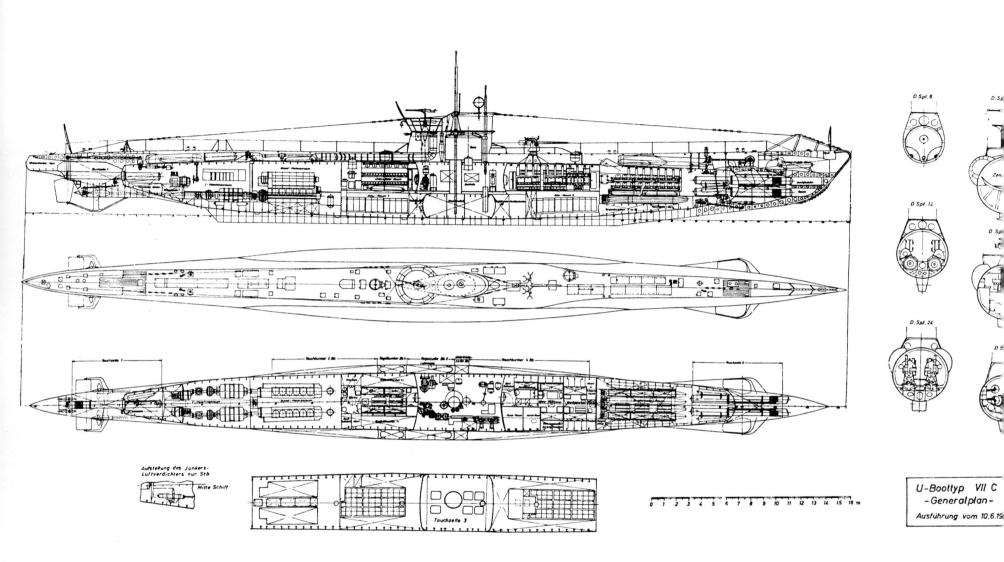

Longitudinal and transverse drawings of Type VII C U-Boats as of June 10, 1940.

Two boats of the 11th Submarine Flotilla at Bergen, Norway. From there they saw action against the British
PQ and QP convoys.

Superstructures and Armament of Type VII C U-Boats

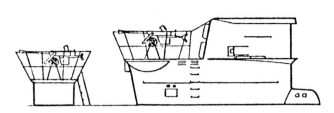

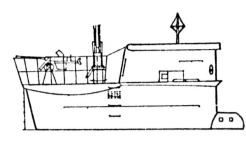

U-84 (VII B) with raised Flak
position behind bridge 1943
2 x 20mm C/38 in LC 30/37

U-81 (VII C) with
enlarged
bridge 1943
Mediterranean
2 x 1.32 cm Breda
twin,
1 x 20mm C/38 in LC
30/37

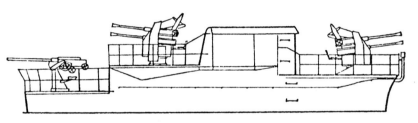

U-441 (U-Flak I)
2 x 20mm quad 38/43 U
1 x 37mm SKC/30 U in LC/39

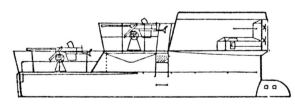

Type VII C with "winter garden"
bridge revision II, 1943
2 x 20mm C/38 in LC 30/37

There were other combinations of weapons.

VII C 1944-45 version
2 x 20mm twin 38 M/II
in double LM 43 U
1 x 37mm M 42 U in LM 42
U

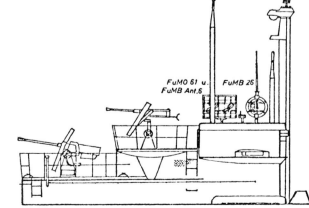

A Type VII C U-Boat arrives at Brest flying three victory pennants.

The battles of the submarines against British convoys in the Arctic Ocean was especially difficult and demanding because of the extreme weather conditions. Right: Very low temperatures turned the boats into ice-covered monsters; towers, guns and everything else were covered with ice. The decks of the boats looked like glittering skating rinks. Stepping on them meant risking one's life.

20mm Flak 38 guns were mounted in C 30/37 naval mounts on both sides. A special Flak setup was built on U-441, built by Schichau at Danzig. It included two quadruple 20mm Flak 38/43 guns and one 37mm Flak 30 in C 39 naval mounts. This strong anti-aircraft armament, though, could not save the boat from destruction by bombs from a British bomber with a Polish crew in the English Channel on June 18, 1944. The following types of anti-aircraft armament were introduced in 1944-45:

Above: A VII C boat is loaded with torpedoes for its next assignment. Upper and lower right: The crew of a Junkers Ju 88 A-4 of Lehrgeschwader (Instructional Squadron) 1 took these pictures while observing the departure of a German U-Boat from Piraeus, the harbor of Athens.

Numerous submarines were transferred to the Mediterranean to support the operations of the *Afrika-Korps*. Several of the boats were lost on the way. The main German U-Boat base was the Italian port of La Spezia.

Left page: U-407 (Type VII C) at La Spezia, April 1944. After the close of operations in North Africa, the boat was transferred to the Aegean Sea. There it was sunk by the British warships ''Troubridge'', ''Terpsichore'' and ''Garland'' near the island of Melos on September 19, 1944.

Above: A VII C boat leaves the quay in Bergen.

Below: U-407 during trimming tests off La Spezia in March of 1943.

Kapitänleutnant Topp was the first commander of the VII C boat U-552, built at the Blohm & Voss yards. *Kptlt.* Topp (with white cap) is talking with his watch officer here. Note the MG 15 visible behind them. U-552 was scuttled by its crew at Wilhelmshaven on May 2, 1945.

Below: The submarines' helpers included the sea-emergency Dornier Do 24 flying boats. Here the flying boat was called on to fly a sick man to the hospital as soon as possible. On the other hand, U-Boats sometimes picked up downed aviators who had been rescued by the flying boats.

Right page: The Type IX boats were bigger than the VII boats and thus able to handle long-distance operations in the South Atlantic, Indian Ocean and off the American coast. Sometimes they also supplied the smaller VII C boats (U-37, Type IX A, at Lorient, October 22, 1940.

In September of 1943, U-235, 236 and 237 were the first boats to be fitted with snorkels that made it possible for them to stay under the surface and still use their Diesel engines. The last VII C boats were built with a stronger pressure hull to be able to reach a greater diving depth. This idea was already at hand when the war broke out, but it was actually used only in 1941, and thus these boats were designated VII C/42. By strengthening the pressure hull, the normal diving depth could be extended to 120 meters and the fighting depth from 165 to 200 meters. The VII C boat U-995 reached a depth of 240 meters without suffering any damage.

Developed from Type VII C were:
VII F U-213 to 218: Optional use as torpedo or mine carriers (14 T+15 mines or 39 mines)

VII F U-1059 to 1062: Torpedo carrier (30 torpedoes!)

How great a role the VII C boats played in fighting against enemy shipping may be seen from the following: From March 16-20, 1943 the largest convoy battle of World War II took place when the British convoys SC 122 and HX 229 were attacked. 42 German U-Boats took part, divided into three groups, "Dränger", "Raubgraf" and "Stürmer" The following boats (commanders' names in parentheses) had success: U-91 (Wackerling), U-221 (Trojer), U-228 (Christophersen), U-305 (Bahr), U-333 (Schwaff), U-338 (Kinzel), U-384 (von Rosenberg), U-435 (Strehlow), U-441 (K. Hartmann), U-523 (Pietsch), U-527 (Uhlig), U-600 (Zurmühlen), U-603 (Bertelsmann), U-608 (Struckmeier), U-631 (Krüger), U-663 (Schmidt), U-665 (Haupt), U-666 (Engel), U-758 (Manseck). In all, these boats sank 21 ships with 140,942 tons. Of these boats, only U-523 and U-527 were Type IX C 40, all the others were Type VII C.

Above: In July 1942, the IX C boat U-154 met the VII C boat U-564 west of the Antilles and supplied it with fuel and torpedoes. Only in this way was it possible to use the VII C boats off the American coast.

Right: Festooned with decorations, U-203 (VII C) returned to its support base at Brest in July of 1942 after successful operations. The commander wears a white cap.

Right page: The men who put out from Brest in U-203 on April 3, 1943 knew for sure that they would need a lot of luck if they were to return. But they did not escape their fate: On April 25, 1943 the boat was spotted by aircraft of the Coastal Command of the Royal Air Force and attacked with bombs. HMS "Biter" and HMS "Pathfinder" then destroyed the boat with depth charges.

In the bow torpedo room of a VII C boat. At the St. Nazaire base, the torpedo is drawn out of the tube for checking.

After being checked, the torpedo is slid back into the tube and the tube is carefully closed.

Above: The training of U-Boat crews was done at the Danzig U-Boat School and at other bases. Here a new class reports to the school commander.

Conditions were always very cramped inside a U-Boat. Then too, the air could not always be purified by cruising on the surface. The cold, damp air left many survivors with rheumatism.

Upper left: The commander has let a war correspondent take his place at the periscope to film a visible target.

Left: The man at the group listening device (GHG) had an important job on a submarine. He followed the run of a torpedo with a stopwatch after it was fired. If the torpedo ran longer than the necessary time for the distance, a miss was recorded. A certain unreliability of German torpedoes turned many a promising shot to a miss.

U-101 (VII B) as a school ship in the Baltic Sea.

The end. On the left page, a Catalina flying boat makes a low-level attack on a U-Boat heavily armed with anti-aircraft guns. This page shows the Canadian corvette "Chilliwake" (left) and frigates "St. Catharines" and "Chaudiere" fighting against a German U-Boat. The boat was compelled by depth charges to surface and surrender.

U744 6 March 1944 HX280

When the Coastal Command of the Royal Air Force began in 1942 to use aircraft more intensively against submarines, the situation became critical for the U-Boats in the Atlantic. The Allies developed their U-Boat defenses, particularly through the use of radar, to the extent that U-Boats scarcely had a chance any more. At first the British carried out anti-submarine operations with American Lockheed "Hudson" planes, and later the Consolidated "Catalina" flying boats were added. The Cataline Mark III and later types carried very high-quality radar equipment, to which many a VII C boat fell victim, quite apart from the devices on board the Allied convoy escort ships.

In conclusion, the achievement of a VII A boat at the beginning of the war deserves to be noted. On September 17, 1939 the commander of U-29, *Kapitänleutnant* Schuhart, spotted the 22,500-ton British aircraft carrier "Courageous" at the west end of the English Channel. After a two-hour chase, he was able to sink the carrier with two torpedoes at 7:50 P.M. This was the first British warship that was sunk by the German Navy in World War II. The U-Boat was scuttled off Flensburg on May 4, 1945.

Technical Data • U-Boat Type VII

Series	A	B	C	C 42	D	F
Size, cubic meters	626/915	753/1040	769/1010	999/1050	965/1285	1084/1345
Length, meters	64.5	66.5	67.1	68.7	76.9	77.6
Diameter, meters	5.9/4.7	6.2/4.7	6.2/4.7	6.8/5.0	6.4/4.7	7.3/4.7
Draught, meters	4.4/9.5	4.7/9.5	4.8/9.6	4.8/9.6	5.0/9.7	4.9/9.6
Horsepower	2100/750	2800/750	2800/750	2700/750	2800/750	2800/750
Speed, knots	16/8	17.2/8	17/6.6	16.7/7.6	16/7.3	16.9/7.9
Diving depth, meters	100 (200)	100 (200)	150 (280)	280 (400)	100 (200)	100 (200)
Oil, tons	67	108	114	180	170	199
Crew	44	44	44	45	44	46
Armament	4 BTR	4 BTR	4 BTR	Same as C	Same as C	4 BTR
	1 HTR	1 HTR	1 HTR	but 4x20mm		1 HTR
	11 T	12 T	14 T Od.			39 T
	1x88mm	1x88mm	14 M			2x20mm
	1x20mm	1x37mm	1x88mm			
		2x20mm	1x37mm			
			2x20mm			
Manufacturers	Deschimag	Krupp	Krupp	Same as C	Krupp	Krupp
	Krupp	Vulcan	Vulcan		only 6 built	only 4 built
		Flender	Flender			
			Howaldt			
			Stülcken			
			Schichau			
			Neptun			
			Nordsee			
			Danzig			
			B & V			
			Deschimag			
			Flensburg			

Code: BTR = bow torpedo tubes, HTR = stern torpedo tube, T = torpedoes carried.

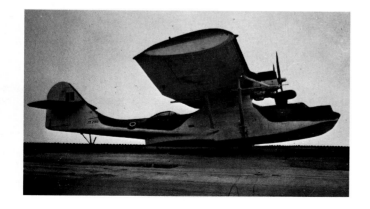

Left: Among the most dangerous opponents of the German U-Boats were the Consolidated "Catalina" flying boats equipped with the most modern radar equipment that spotted the boats in any weather and even underwater and then directed the sub-chasers of the Allied navies. Escapes were rare.

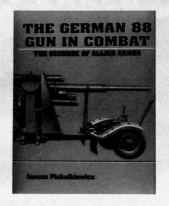
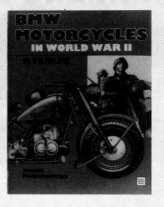